the Bedeviled DICTIONARY

A LEXICON OF WICKED WORD PLAY

by **L.K. PETERSON**

& **MARTIN KOZLOWSKI**

All illustrations by Martin Kozlowski

Thanks to Barbara Winard for editorial assistance

L.K. Peterson

L.K. Peterson's books include *Fairly Grim Tales, The Da Vinci Cold, Talk to the Hair, The 2012 Doomsday Planner, Further Adventures: Now What Anthology #1, Political Animals: Now What Anthology #2*, and *Karen in Wonderland*. He is also entirely to blame for the website *Ant Farmer's Almanac*.

Martin Kozlowski

Martin Kozlowski has chronicled the social and political scenes in a wide range of publications. He art directs the weekly editorial illustration service at inxart.com and is co-publisher at nowwhatmedia.com. Samples of his illustration and comics work are available at martinkozlowski.com.

Introduction

Have you ever noticed an unfamiliar word or expression suddenly popping up everywhere and wondered 'What's that supposed to mean?' Or, conversely, have you encountered some emerging mishegoss for which there was no existing word? If so, *the Bedeviled Dictionary* is for you.

Language is made up of words and words are, well, made up. Think about it. At some point, a cave person went from waving off rival hunters with menacing grunts to saying — and we are paraphrasing here — "Go find your own woolly mammoth, I saw this one first!" Whether the intruders understood what these new noises meant is anybody's guess, but between the expressive delivery and the speaker's brandishing a club big enough to bring down a woolly mammoth, they got the gist. Over time, this message evolved* into the more succinct and far scarier, "You'll be hearing from my lawyers."

---

*   Readers who reject the concept of evolution can skip the rest of this introduction and just go straight to the jokes.

Shakespeare alone invented some 1,700 words and phrases. Honestly, it's a wonder he had time for anything else. America's lexicon expanded faster than manifest destiny, and new words continue to enter the language every day or so in response to societal trends, technological innovation, fun, profit, or somebody just having too much time on their hands.

The meaning of words can change too. This may happen gradually or in the blink of an eye while your back is turned (providing that you blinked during that time). The new becomes the norm, the norm becomes old hat and then new again when old hats become trendy.

Offered in the spirit of Ambrose Bierce, the godfather of cryptolexography, this dictionary is a collection of newly minted neologisms along with irreverent redefinitions of the current crop of buzzwords, slang, and weaselspeak waiting for us out there every day.

—The Editors

I Have No Words!

Acceptionalism

Coming to grips with the idea we aren't necessarily all that superior to everyone else in the world and maybe we should dial it down a notch.

Acid Reflux Flashback

Unpleasant reminder of what you probably shouldn't have had for lunch.

Ad Hock

When you go into debt buying commercial time.

Adjectify

To make an advertisement from something that was never meant to be an advertisement.

Aftershokkenfreude

Sense of joy and relief upon realizing that last jolt wasn't a whole new earthquake.

¡A.I. Caramba!

Exclamation when experiencing a disaster caused by artificial intelligence.

Airier Rug

A well-ventilated hairpiece.

Alleged

A truth not yet proven in court.

Alter Khakis

1) Chinos for old guys.
2) Old Chinos.

Alternative Fax

Messages sent without a grain of truthiness.

Amex Predator

The guy at a business lunch waving around his Centurion Black card in a show of dominance.

Anormaly

When the deviation becomes the same old same old.

ALTER KHAKIS

Anthropomorphize

To insult animals by projecting human traits and characteristics onto them.

Antillectual

Hostility toward critical thinking and fact-gathering — and the rejection of any conclusions or ideas that result from it.

Antivexxer

Someone in denial that they're the one who's annoying.

Antsysocial

When one is extremely nervous at parties.

App Nauseum

The realization that you've never used half the apps on your phone and you've forgotten what most of them even do.

Appnea

When an app stops working momentarily, then suddenly starts up again for no good reason.

Aptitude Adjustment

Manipulating school curriculum to raise test score averages.

Arrefutable

Statement that cannot be disproved when made by a pirate.

Artificial Swedener

1) Assemble-it-yourself furniture not from Ikea.

2) Socialized medicine outside of Scandinavia.

Artisanal

A distinctive and high-quality food item made using traditional methods and in such small batches that it will be sold out by the time you get there.

Auteur-Erotic Asphyxiation

Cinephile's breathless praise of their favorite director.

Authentic

Newly applicable prefix for anything not generated by AI; comparable to "Analog" clock or "Acoustic" guitar.

Avattoir

End of the line for gamers' digital persona.

Backstreet Bias

Skittish drivers' tendency to avoid highways.

Balloon Animal Farm

"Air Good, Helium Better."

Bandwidth

Slang term for IQ, usually applied in a derogatory manner, e.g., "Harrison hasn't got nearly enough bandwidth for this assignment, but he is the boss's nephew."

Barbecuecore

Hyper-macho accessorizing of suburban dads outdoor grilling experience, including spatula and tongs made from weapons-grade Molybdenum steel, charcoal lighter fluid distilled from army surplus napalm, blast-resistant Oakley sunglasses, and a Kevlar® apron that says, "Kiss the Chef!"

Bask Separatist

Nude beachgoer who insists on having at least ten paces between their towel and the next nearest naturist's.

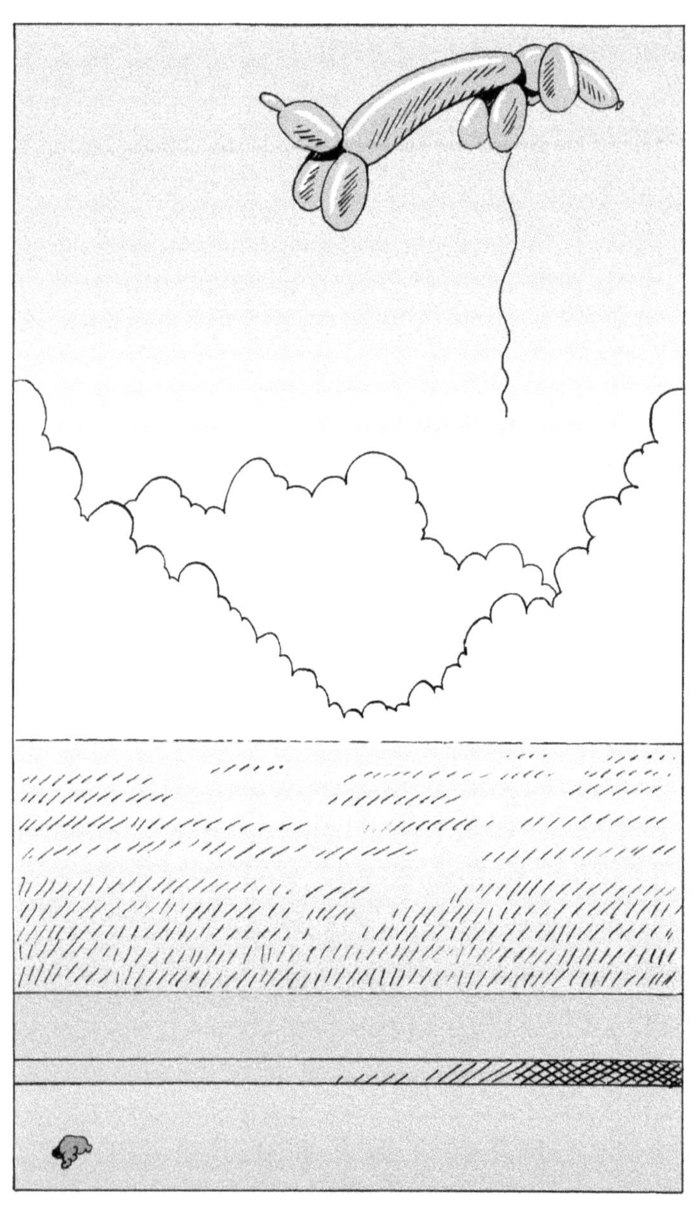

BALLOON ANIMAL FARM

Bdoomers

Americans born between 1946 and 1964 convinced that every new thing they don't like or understand is ushering in the end of civilization.

Berserk de Soleil

Irrational behavior associated with sunstroke.

Betaphor

Early test version of a metaphor, e.g., dingy sheep of the family.

Bierce Goggles

Superior bullshit detection abilities, with possessor often accused of being cynical by those whose bullshit has been detected.

Big Data

Name of overbearing robot character in AI-generated *CAD on a Hot Tin Roof* reimagining of Tennessee Williams' work.

Bipartisan

Strategically switching party affiliation to sink or support a primary candidate.

Bisect

Insect that swings both ways.

Bitchcoin

What you'll call it once the whole scheme collapses and your investment has vanished.

Black-Eyed Peace

Handshake after a fistfight.

Blue Suede Schmooze

Gathering of pre-army Elvis fans.

Bobby Positive

[British colloquial] Pro-police.

Boeing

The sound made by a loose jet part hitting the ground.

Bogus Points

Wild accusation that forces a debate opponent to use up valuable time refuting it.

Bon-Bon Mot

When you think of a witty remark but have a mouthful of chocolate.

Bone Appetit!

Cannibal's pre-dinner interjection.

Booyah Base

Group of over-excitable bros who triumphantly cheer their slightest accomplishments.

Borista

Server at Russian coffee bar.

Bosom Bubbes

Well-endowed grandmothers who unselfconsciously expose a little too much décolletage.

Botchulism

Restaurant serving a dish containing ingredients a diner has told them they're allergic to.

Brontesaurus

Literate dinosaur whose arms are too short to reach the keyboard.

Bum Rap

Hip-hop for hobos.

Burnt Umbrage

A grievance that has become a grudge.

Butt Dial

Ancient device for predicting full moons.

C-Spanx

TV coverage of Congress edited to make members look less embarrassing.

Candiose

Epically sweet.

Canvas Stretcher

Knocked-out boxer.

Carb Uncle

Adult relative who takes nieces and nephews out for pizza regardless of the occasion.

Carnegie Haul

Performer's percentage of the gate at a prestigious venue.

Carp Diem

Kvetch of the day.

Carterize

To blame someone for everything that's wrong, regardless of their responsibility for or ability to control any of it; to designate a fall guy.

Catastrophonic

Symphony played by a terrible orchestra.

Catatonic

Comfortably numb, trancelike state induced by binging on internet cat videos.

Chekhov's Helicopter

If introduced in an action movie's first 20 minutes, it must crash dramatically in the final 20 minutes.

Cheesed Dip

Angry goofball.

Chin Chiller

Removal of a full beard.

Chick Magnate

1) Publisher of a men's magazine.

2) Successful poultry farmer.

Chump Change

When a con artist chooses a different mark.

Circuitous Roots

A tangled family tree.

Circumspectator

Someone with a good view from a safe distance.

Ciscombobulated

To be flummoxed by the idea of gender fluidity.

Cite Seeing

Reading the footnotes.

Clickbait

The definition will shock you!

Cocktail Frank

That guy you always see at the end of
the bar.

Cognitive Dissidents

Those who insist they saw something
completely different than what the rest
of us just saw.

Coin Op

Process of devising a neologism.

Coincidolences

When you run into someone at a
funeral you haven't seen for a long time
and who you didn't realize also knew
the deceased.

Comboverture

Period during which a bald man lets the remaining hair on one side of his head grow long enough to reach across to the hair remaining on the other side.

Collared Greens

Environmental activists who have been arrested.

Comida and Tragedy

Disastrous meal at a Mexican restaurant.

Commentater

Someone with strong opinions about potatoes.

Conk Shell

Boxing slang for noggin.

Coup d'Foie Gras

To sucker punch a goose.

COMIDA and TRAGEDY

Cringe

The appropriate response upon first hearing a verb used as a noun.

Crocks

Knock-off of the name-brand footwear.

Crud'état

What happens when a charcuterie platter is added to an all-vegetable buffet table.

Crunge

Grunge music that hasn't aged well.

Cryptocurrency

Fake money you can't use paid for with real money you'll never get back.

Cuddlefish

Adorable-if-kind-of-clingy addition to any aquarium.

Curfluffle

Dust-up in a dog park.

Cynic Boom

Proliferation of pessimists.

Cyberputz

Online jerk.

Cymbalism

To emphasize your point with a rim shot.

Debtor's Prism

Perspective of someone mortgaged up to their eyeballs.

Delululemon

The mistaken belief that you look good in tight-fitting athleisure wear.

Denaliism

Refusing to call it anything but Mt. McKinley.

Dickensian

Characteristic behavior of dicks.

Distributed Cloud

Rain. Or, in the digital world, a service that pisses down your back and tells you it's rain.

Doppleradarganger

When the weather someplace else is just like it is where you are.

Dreambloat

When a youthful idol packs on some pounds.

Drill Down

The process of finding the root cause of an organizational problem; those tasked with the search are motivated to "keep digging" until the source of the problem is found to not be anyone in upper management.

Dud Reckoning

Accurate review of a lousy film or TV show.

Dude Diligence

Continuing to abide.

Dumbosthenes

One who argues against self-determination.

Dupelicate

To be duped by a dupe.

Echolade

Praise for the panderer from those pandered to.

Economicull

To retain profit by cutting staff.

Ecoillogical

Knowing something's bad for the environment and doing it anyway.

Edgelord

Gratuitous provocateur. A narcissistic troll whose only agenda is to bring attention to themself. An asshole.

Effluence

An overabundance of swear words in a piece of recorded entertainment.

Ehfluencer

Less-than-persuasive social media marketer.

Elitist

Anyone in a tax bracket higher than you.

Emcee Hammer

Gavel used by a Master of Ceremonies.

Emonacon

Enigmatic emoji.

En Pointe of No Return

Ballet position just prior to a fall.

Enviralmentalist

One who studies social media.

Errorstocracy

The folly of ascribing superiority to heredity.

Escargauche

Pointing out they're eating snails to someone who didn't know beforehand.

EMONACON

Evidense

Bogus proof gleaned from a 30-second Google search or hearsay from a work friend's cousin's neighbor's stepbrother who knows a guy who "was totally there when it happened."

Existenchal Threat

Horrible smell that you're sure will kill you if you don't get away from it fast enough.

Existential Dreadlocks

Clueless white teenager's culturally appropriated hairstyle that they believe displays solidarity but, in fact, only makes them targets of campus pot dealers and narcs.

Exposure Therapy

Controversial mental health treatment touting the psychological benefits of exhibitionism.

Fad Accompli

A craze that's run its course.

Faschismo

Showy display of manly chest-thumping
that signals the intent to dominate
by brute force or at least the threat
thereof.

Fearal

Easily startled.

Festidious

To celebrate any and every holiday on
the calendar.

Fibonacci, Alfredo

Famous mathematician's cousin; lousy
with numbers, but a terrific cook.

Film-Flam

Movie business marketing bullshit.

FIBONACCI, ALFREDO

Flaccid Rock

Mopey pop music characterized by whiny vocalizations and self-pitying lyrics, lacking any of the gritty self-awareness, raw emotion or humor found in blues, r&b, soul or country music.

Flap Flop

Unsuccessful attempt at creating a scandal.

Fourbearance

When three bears just aren't enough.

Frug State

Nervous disorder characterized by rhythmic shifting of the hips.

Funding Fathers

Sugar Daddies.

Gadzilla

G-Rated monster that isn't very scary.

Gamboling Problem

Unable to frolic without tripping over one's own feet.

Game Changer!

Overused expression regarding something that changes nothing about something that isn't a game.

Geez Force

A system of measuring how much effort and noise it takes an old guy to get out of his chair. Not to be confused with "Gee Force," that measures the emotional intensity behind an exclamation of the phrase, "Aw, gee."

Ghoul-Oriented

Workers in the supernatural-industrial complex.

Gilt Trip

Nouveau riche spending spree.

Girl Dinner

Hors d'oeuvres instead of a meal; aka "Snacking," "Grazing," "Don't feel like cooking." Not to be confused with "Girl Boss Dinner," which involves an expense account.

Glamoflage

Dressing like you're on the way to *The Hunger Games* opening ceremony.

Goombahlaya

Dish favored by New Orleans gangsters.

Gravitoss

Finale of vehement Thanksgiving dinner argument.

Guillotonne

Unit of measuring overkill (metric system only).

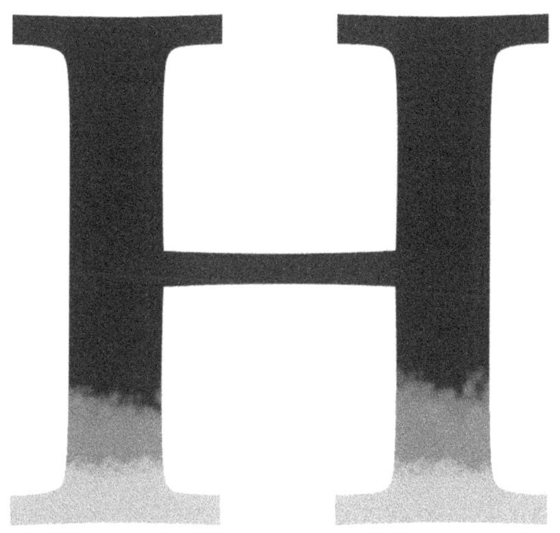

Haha Moment

When you realize something is funny.

Halacious

Impacted disastrously by a computer error.

Halalacious

Subpar Arab street food.

Hallucinotion

Figment of the collective imagination reacted to as if real.

Half-Baked Alaska

What tourists should expect on an eco-cruise to what's left of the 49th state's glaciers.

Hashstag

A meal with just the boys.

Having a Moment

Flash in the pan, flavor of the month. Something destined for three to five minutes of fame, tops.

Heard Mentality

Demographic group's belief that cultural validation is best achieved through a trifecta of being pandered to by Madison Avenue, Hollywood, and grandstanding politicians.

Hedgetate

To avoid making a difficult decision; what one does when there isn't a 10-foot-pole handy; i.e., The Supreme Court *hedgetated* about ruling on gay marriage.

Heirloon

Descendant who loses family fortune on some crazy scheme.

Heisman Principle

Past performance does not guarantee future success.

HEISMAN PRINCIPLE

Hip Displacement

When pioneering hipsters are priced out of a neighborhood they made desirable. (see also; Indegentry)

Hippity-Hoppity

Rap music for preschoolers.

Hohumicide

A murder too mundane to be the subject of a podcast.

Hokum-Pocus

Illusory or nonsensical distraction to trick you into an unthinking emotional response.

Holistic

Taking into account an entity's totality when evaluating issues. In a business setting, this allows for expanding the

field of potential scapegoats far outside
the core management team handling a
project.

Holy Roiler

One whose antagonism is fueled by
religious fervor.

Howdy Duty

Greeter's job at a big box store.

Howl-Too Book

A guide to bonding with your dog.

Humbugle

Nickname for kazoo.

Hypenotized

Semi-trancelike state induced by
prolonged exposure to relentless
overstatement and exaggeration,

causing sensory overload and resulting in numb indifference to any and all further input.

Hyperboleak

Warning sign your vast exaggeration is about to deflate.

Hyperbollox

[British usage] Extremely nonsensical; i.e., "In hindsight, the arguments for Brexit seem like *hyperbollox*."

Hyperlocal

Artisanal items made from ingredients sourced within the same zip code.

Hyperthetical Question

The opposite of a hypothetical question, especially if asked very quickly.

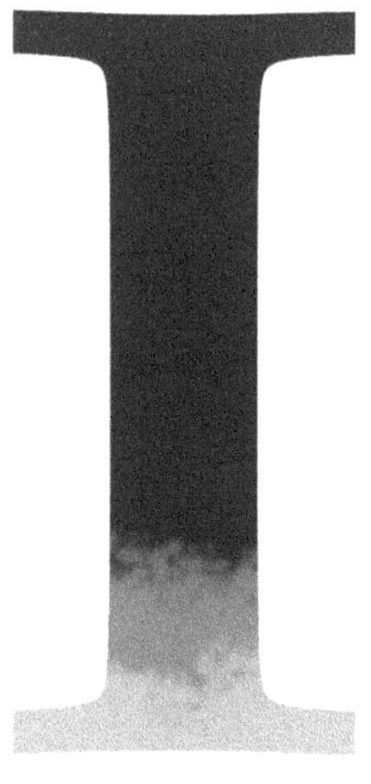

Iambec

Something we imagine Beck says a lot.

Icklectic

Diverse collection of distasteful objects gathered from a wide variety of sources.

Idiolatry

The worship by idiots of an even bigger idiot.

Impossible Nothingburger

Pale imitation of the not-real thing.

Incelent

Characteristic attitude of the snotty, single, horny and alone.

Incentivize

To wield bribes or threats as motivation for employees to work weekends.

Indigentry

Long-time residents of a newly gentrified neighborhood who get no benefit from it and now pay $12.50 for a cup of coffee.

Inimal

Animal that lives indoors.

Inner Circle

Close associates who'll get the biggest book advance for their tell-all about how awful you are.

Intersectionality

Acknowledgment that every person's opinion is formed through a unique set of individual experiences — frequently including them having been dropped on the head as an infant.

Intractorpull

In too deep for any way out.

Itty Biddy

Little old lady with a sharp tongue.

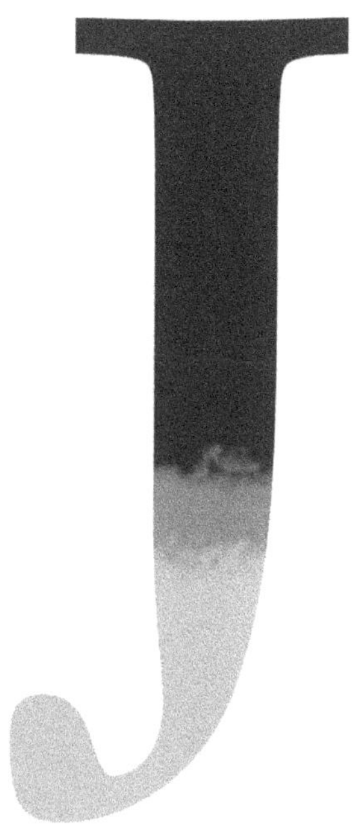

J'acuzzi

Judgy hot tub.

Janky Ingenuity

Clever invention that makes a lot of noise and leaks oil.

Jean Splicing

Pre-distressing denim.

Jerryatric

Comedian's later, lesser material but still considered works of genius in France.

Jest Blue

Off-color joke.

Jumbo Scrimp

Strenuously penny pinching to save up for large expenditure, ex., a mortgage down payment.

Jurisprunence

Selectively scaling back established law.

JURISPRUNENCE

Kaddishack

Thankfully never-produced star vehicle for Jackie Mason.

Kaffeclutch

Holding on to that first cup for dear life until the caffeine kicks in.

Kakistophony

Sound made by a crooked government caught in the act.

Ken Buddhism

Coming to terms with being a beta male.

Kitsch Lorraine

Neighbor of ours. You don't know her. Collects way too many garden gnomes.

Knight-Erron't

Someone who, in hindsight, should never have been knighted in the first place.

Kuraçaoa

Japanese liqueur.

Labradoor

Special entrance for medium-to-large canines.

Laminatation

Expression of grief that one's floors aren't real wood.

Leaf Blower

Someone adept at shifting blame or quickly making their problem somebody else's.

Leche Libre

Lactose-intolerant Mexican wrestling.

Line-Item Patriots

Constitutional cherry pickers. (see also; Originalish)

Lingua Pranca

Universally understood practical joke.

Lip-Sinking

Continuing to speak after you've said something stupid and just making it worse.

Lobstertrician

Shellfish specialist in a seafood restaurant.

Loggerhythm

Pace maintained by successful woodmen.

Logistics

The go-to excuse for why something is behind schedule.

Loose Canon

What's left after a fantasy film franchise has been rebooted.

Malodor Brides

Iffy wife-import business.

Manic Pedi

Frenetic foot job.

Maniker

Anachronistic male-to-male form of address: ace, big guy, boyo, bub, buddy, buddy-boy, doc, fella, joe, mac, mister, pal, sport, etc.;

a) when preceded by "Hey," acknowledges lack of familiarity or mild disdain or disrespect,

b) when preceded by "Listen up," indicates open hostility if not a direct threat.

Manstipulation

It's only okay if a man does it.

Mayan Culpa

What the 2012 Doomsday predictors did after December 21, 2012.

Mechanical Bull

Robocalls.

Mehta

A profound lack of enthusiasm about your own indifference.

Memery Hole

Where ephemeral internet content goes after its 15 minutes of fame are up.

Men Buddhism

To contemplate the sound of one cylinder misfiring.

Menschplaining

1) A nice person telling someone how they do it.

2) Telling a nice person that they're nice.

Mental Blog

Utterly insane online posts.

Metafive

Metaphor so overused (i.e., "Worse than Hitler!") as to render the speaker's argument dismissible as hyperbole.

Mettle Fatigue

When it's alls youse can stands, cuz youse can't stands no more!

Mexican Hate Dance

1. Punitive steps taken by US politicians along the southern border.

2. Performative appearances on southern border by virulently anti-immigrant politicians.

Micro Bro

The shortest guy in a group; often the designated wingman.

Midlift crisis

Weightlifter's anxiety before jerking.

Millennial Buddhism

Phone app for mindfulness; premium subscribers achieve nirvana without ads.

Milk of Amnesia

Memory wipe-strength cream-based cocktail.

Moderation

Unfashionable notion that avoiding extremes and/or knowing when to stop is somehow a good thing. (see also, Nuance.)

Mongrel Hoard

A dog walker's bevy of mutts.

Monk Mode

To focus intensely on a single work task by aggressively cutting out all distractions. If done while humming Gregorian chants and wearing an itchy hooded robe, the phrase indicates that you're going straight from the office to a Renaissance Fair.

Month-to-Month Resuscitation

Lifestyle-sustaining payment made every 30 days, e.g., alimony, pension, social security.

Motorfied

Deeply embarrassed by one's wheels.

Multi-Tisking

Middle-aged adult's ability to simultaneously disapprove of several behaviors of younger generation.

Musky

The distinct aroma of money and EV batteries going up in smoke.

Myhilism

Lack of belief in oneself.

Nachoos

Just like regular nachos but with too much black pepper.

Naderp

When an accomplished person's dumbass late-career statements or actions overshadow their prior work, rendering it a footnote to the stupid shit they just said or did; i.e., Ralph Nader. (see also, Rudymental)

Nahpology

Genuine regret over being forced to insincerely apologize.

Nana Technology

Any pre-digital device that young people are ill-equipped to operate; e.g., rotary dial phone, manual transmission.

Napnea

Attempted snooze that keeps being interrupted.

Neofarious

One who gleefully breaks rules, laws, and traditions of conduct and dares you to do anything about it.

Neologin

Newly updated password.

Newstalgia

Longing for the near future.

Next Generation

The only true rival to The Original Series.

NFT

WTF?

Ninny State

We're livin' in it, baby.

Noir'easter

Brooding stormfront propelled to its grim, inescapable destiny by dark secrets and a troubled past.

Nomad

For now, yeah.

Noncompoop

Not-too-bright sergeant.

Nookie Mistake

Amorous misstep.

Non-Stick Irony

When reaction to the difference between expectation and reality evokes little more than a shrug.

NOIR'EASTER

Nonumental

Way less impressive than expected, if not a colossal disappointment: "Not really such a big deal."

Norsassist

The guy who polishes Thor's hammer.

Nuance

Intellectual/philosophical concept hunted to extinction by those with no use for it. (see also, Moderation.)

Oh, Currant!

What you say when you realize it's not blackberry jam like you thought it was.

Occam's Raisinets

They're just raisins.

Offshore Accountant

What you've got when you call your tax guy and can barely hear him over the sound of crashing waves and Jimmy Buffet music in the background.

OK Chorale

So-so choir.

OnlyFlans

Amateur food porn site.

Ononism

Shameless pleasuring of oneself in the recording studio.

Oofemism

To downplay the severity of a stumble, "I'm fine. Hardly hurts at all. It looked way worse than it was."

Oopsy Daisy

Botched floral delivery.

Opp Sit

Take a chair across from.

Originalish

Someone fiercely devoted to most of the Constitution; Amendments, after the second one, not so much. (see also, Line-Item Patriots)

Over Awwed

Exaggerated, enthusiastic cooing over an average-looking baby.

Paid Partner Legislation

A proposed bill that primarily benefits the proposer's benefactors.

Pan Handler

Short-order saucier.

Paravegetarian

One who eats only animals that eat only vegetables.

Parawassailing

Lip-synching to Christmas carols.

Pawntificate

Opinion presented as fact and intended to provoke the listener into actions beneficial to the speaker but not to themselves.

PedEx

When it absolutely, positively has to get there on foot.

PEDEX

Perfumative

Covering up an unpleasant odor with an expensive one.

Perp-Plex

To annoy, befuddle, or confuse a criminal in the middle of their crime.

Petterphile

Animal lover who can't keep their hands off other people's doggos.

Pharm Team

Public officials working to protect pharmaceutical companies from the public.

Phenomenot

Something that falls far short of its hype.

Pie Curious

Sure, you wanted a birthday *cake* but, you're open to new experiences.

Pinyaddayadda

To continue whacking at an already split open and emptied-of-candy papier-mâché donkey.

Pith Poor

Tedious, rambling, drawn-out.

Pizzazz Parlor

Advertising agency.

Plaguerisim

When an epidemic mimics the symptoms of one that came before.

Plebe Bargain

Military academy's gift shop sale.

Plebexcite

Amusement for the hoi polloi.

Poll Results

When more people whose opinion you asked for agree with you than those whose didn't.

Pollyamorous

Being romantically involved with more than one parrot at the same time.

Posthates

Nasty online comments.

Post-Postmodernism

Six syllables in search of a definition.

Pro Former

Arch conservative.

Pulling a Hammy

Overacting.

Puppywhipped

When you have your dog right where it wants you.

PSINO

Public Servant in Name Only.

Pundit

Having successfully made a pun.

Push Up Bro

Male gym rat.

Pzygotic

Agitation resulting from unsuccessful attempts to conceive.

Quack

Unlicensed waterfowl veterinarian.

Quarrantino

Forcibly isolated with only the films *Pulp Fiction, Reservoir Dogs,* and *Kill Bill* (Vols. 1 & 2) to pass the time.

Queasynart

Gas station gastronomy.

Quench

Barmaid at a Ren Faire.

Queryless

Demanding answers for which there are no questions.

Quiet Quitting

Giving only as good as you're getting paid for.

Quintessance

Deep-seated hatred of sharks.

Ragamuffin

Muffin made from recyclable materials.

RAM Sleep

What happens after you've counted enough sheep to finally nod off.

Rantatouille

A well-prepared and carefully arranged fulmination without any meat.

Reductio et Absurdum

First century AD Roman comedy duo whose career was cut short when, while on tour in Pompeii, Mt. Vesuvius erupted in the middle of their signature routine, "Quis est in primo."

Reese's Monkey

Primate with a sweet tooth.

Relative Tumidity

Situationally appropriate level of sexual arousal.

Rental Case

Pathological aversion to ownership.

Resaidavist

Someone who repeatedly talks too much.

Retrow

To go backwards in a dinghy.

Revisionist History

Fan fictionalization.

Rinoplasty

Procedure necessary to turn moderates to MAGA.

Rizzible

Terms spawned in a media hothouse meth lab ("rizz," "zaddy") that no one has ever needed and never will, but that somehow become hot new buzzwords.

Robusto

Why you need a new robe.

Rom-Con

Movie billed as a romantic comedy that turns out to be neither.

Rudymental

To shit all over your own carefully crafted public image. (see also, Naderp)

Ruff Translation

Ineffectual effort to make sense of your dog's barking.

Sackrosanct

Protected by a reinforced codpiece.

Same Scent Marriage

When both spouses use the same bar of soap.

Sans Sheriff

Lacking any and all oversight or regulation, e.g., a Wild West boomtown.

Santos Clause

When someone tells you who they aren't, believe them.

Scandi Crush

Enthralled with Nordic noir.

Scantily Plaid

A kilt that's way too short.

Schlemeal

Food prepared so badly that, if dropped or spilled, is no big loss.

Schrodinger's Cappuccino

Is it regular or decaf? You can't know till you drink it.

Shvitz Take

To comedically shake off sweat after a steam.

Scuzz and Effect

Disturbed response — ex., cringing, choking or retching — to disgusting behavior.

Seance Quiz

What a medium gives a ghost.

Septic Thanks

Extremely and transparently insincere expression of gratitude.

Shit Sue

To bring suit against a neighbor who let their small dog poop on your property.

SCHRODINGER'S CAPPUCCINO

Shot Clock

Timepiece not worth repairing.

Sidekick Friends Network

A loose affiliation of second bananas.

Simper Fidelis

Half-hearted oath of loyalty.

Sinpatico

Sharing the same vices.

Smithsoniac

Somebody way too enthusiastic about
the Smithsonian.

Snob Sister

Female sibling who can't believe where
you live, what you watch, how you
dress, who you date.

Snort Subject

Joke guaranteed to cause ejection of liquid from nasal cavities.

Snowflak

Snark aimed at the very sensitive.

Soddenfreud

Psychoanalyst who's all wet.

Soap Scum

Daytime TV villain.

Social Justice Worrier

Political progressive concerned they're not doing enough.

Special Interest Groups

The other side's contributors and supporters.

Spitefail

Ineffectual vow of revenge.

Squabble

Argument between young pigeons.

Squirm Count

Tally of uncomfortable situations in an HBO comedy series.

Startup

Early stages of a fledgling enterprise before the founders have been pushed out by the venture capitalists they brought in to keep it going.

Status Cling

Over-identification with social standing one does not currently hold (class, economic, celebrity); applicable to status lost or aspired to.

Steambath Willie

Manspreading in the sauna.

Steampunked

When the finely engraved retro-futuristic pocket watch you bought at Comic-Con turns out to be digital.

Straw Poll

Unstable, unsupportable, highly flammable.

Sub-Bourbon Sprawl

Passed out drunk on the cheap stuff.

Sunk Coast

What your grandchildren will call South Florida.

Supersillious

Stupid but funny.

Surge Pricing

Price gouging done with good PR;
if the PR is really good, it's called
Dynamic Pricing.

Sustainability

Implies environmental awareness, but
it usually means they have enough
capital to just go out and buy more of
anything they need.

Synergy

Reason given for a business venture
that succeeds but no one involved has
any idea why.

Teachable Moment

When a public figure is shocked, shocked! by something to which the only reasonable, commonsense response is, "Well, *duh!*"

Terrible Toos

When the rabble becomes roused.

Texpatriots

Lone Star loyalists eager to secede again.

Thinking Outside the Box

What upper management calls it when one of their own has a wackadoo idea that actually pays off.

Tie Bo

Martial arts-based form of gift wrapping.

Tiery-Eyed

Upper deck ticket holders watchful for ways to work their way down to better seats over the course of the game.

Tilting at Windmills

Specious arguments against any and all renewable resources, i.e., "What happens when it's *not* windy, *huh*? What about *then*?"

Tipping Point

Critical part of formula for calculating gratuity amount.

Tirade Negotiations

Debate over how long a rant may last.

Toryadore

[British slang] To lean right.

Tourist Spout

Glowing reviews by visitors of sites locals avoid.

Trancendentist

Oral surgeon who uses hypnotism instead of anesthesia.

Treacle Down Effect

Tendency of sickly-sweet sentiments to be reshared on social media.

Trenditionalist

One who goes all in on any and every emerging trend.

Triggermarole

Convoluted process of getting even the most minimal gun control legislation passed.

Troll Road

Mythical Trail of Liberal Tears that ends abruptly if you correctly guess the troll's real name.

TRANCENDENTIST

Tropiary

Hedge sculpture depicting a figure of speech.

Truckulence

Stubborn attitude of big rig drivers who refuse to get out of the left lane.

Trumpoline

Multiple sudden and unexpected emotional ups and downs for an extended period of time that, however entertaining at first, results in a perpetual state of exhaustion, i.e., "Dating Pat was like being on a trumpoline with no way off."

U-Boat

Typical question posed by a sailor upon one's first meeting.

Umpathy

Sensitivity towards a game official who's being booed.

Unharolded

Going by "Hal" or just the initial "H".

United Amirites

A bloc of self-satisfied know-it-alls.

Unpacking

Evaluation of a business project gone wrong in which each component of it is examined and blame for its failure is assigned. Pro tip: it will never be the fault of whoever has called the meeting.

Unpresciedented

Something nobody saw coming.

Upshot

Fired into the air.

Verisimplitude

Giving the appearance of being simple.

Vex populi

The complaints of the people.

Vexhator

Someone who acts in an irritating and annoying manner in order to promote or incite hate.

Vexxine

Inoculation against annoyance (a guaranteed Nobel Prize for whoever comes up with one).

Virtue Turn-Signaling

To indicate a dramatic change of opinion.

Volcanic Ass

Extreme gassiness.

Whatabotulism

Toxic condition brought on by the over-exertion of trying to prove others' sins are worse than your own.

Wheelhouse *(That's Right in My…)*

Declaration of the overconfident and overeager; white collar equivalent of, "Hold my beer."

Whys Guy

Philosopher.

Wickyleaks

Candle wax on your tablecloth.

Wide Awoke

The awareness that not everything you don't like is a threat to everything you do like.

Wife-Fi

Spousal ability to remotely detect chores not being done.

Wily Mammoth

Hirsute prehistoric pachyderm clever enough to survive the end of the Ice Age.

Wishywashy

Something you wish had been washed.

Work Smarter

What you're told to do after your department's budget and staff have been cut but you're expected to produce the same amount of work.

Wretched

Unproduced prequel to *Wicked*.

X

Not what it used to be and getting worse every day.

Xanacts

Anti-anxiety behavior modification techniques.

Xenaphobia

Fear of warrior princesses.

Xeroxen

Herd cloned from a single ox.

Xylophobe

Parent of a toddler who's about to "lose" the mallets for their rainbow-colored xylophone pull toy.

XENAPHOBIA

Yachtzee

Dice game in which the winner gets a
boat.

Yahoo

Traditionally first on list of yawhat, yawhere, yawhen, yawhy.

Y'awl

A type of flat-bottom boat propelled with a long pole and generally used in Southern US swamps.

Ye Ha!

The title of Kanye's stand-up comedy or country & western album, whichever comes first.

Yeast Inflection

The point at which you have to decide whether to bake gluten-free.

Yeet Me

Retort to being told you're trusted only as far as you can be thrown.

Yen Buddhism

Pay to Pray.

Yelt

Online review in all caps.

Yore

Often overlooked alternative misspelling of "Your" and "You're."

Yowl

Lesser-known work by Allen Ginsberg about his trip to the dentist.

Yuge

Tremendous. More, perhaps, than anyone has ever seen. Bigly, even.

Zero Dim Sum

Don't worry, there's always more
coming.

Zerox

No copying allowed.

Zilch

What you're left with when your identity's been filched.

Zinger Songwriter

Composer of biting lyrics, e.g., Tom Lehrer, Randy Newman.

Zomba

Fitness program for the walking dead.

Zombiffy

Maybe a zombie. Maybe not.

Zuppehero

Maestro of minestrone.

Zyzzyva

To feel a chill at the bitter end.

Zzzillennial

Sleepy young person.